EXPLORING

WILTS & DORSET

COUNTRY

• A PAST AND PRESENT COMPANION •

33	FOXHOLES (Housing Estate)—STANLEY GREEN—POOLE—HAMWORTHY.	33

Light figures denote a.m. times. Dark figures denote p.m. times.

	NSu	NSu	NSu	NSu	NSu		NSu		NSu		NSu		NSu		NSu		NSu
Foxholes (Housing Estate) dep	...	7 40	8 10	8 40	9 0	9 40	10 0	10 40	11 0	11 40	12 0	12 40	1 0	1 40	2 0	2 40	3 0	3 40	4 0	4 40	5 0
Oakdale School ... ... „	...	7 44	8 14	8 44	9 4	9 44	10 4	10 44	11 4	11 44	12 4	12 44	1 4	1 44	2 4	2 44	3 4	3 44	4 4	4 44	5 4
Stanley Green ... ... „	...	7 45	8 15	8 45	9 5	9 45	10 5	10 45	11 5	11 45	12 5	12 45	1 5	1 45	2 5	2 45	3 5	3 45	4 5	4 45	5 5
Poole Library ... ... „	7 0	7 50	8 20	8 50	9 10	9 50	10 10	10 50	11 10	11 50	12 10	12 50	1 10	1 50	2 10	2 50	3 10	3 50	4 10	4 50	5 10
Hamilton Road (Lake Road) arr	7 10	8 0	8 30	9 0	9 20	10 0	10 20	11 0	11 20	12 0	12 20	1 0	1 20	2 0	2 20	3 0	3 20	4 0	4 20	5 0	5 20

	NSu		NSu						
Foxholes (Housing Estate) dep	5 40	6 0	6 40	7 0	8 0	9 0	9 10	10 0	10 55	...
Oakdale School ... ... „	5 44	6 4	6 44	7 4	8 4	9 4	10 4	10 59	...
Stanley Green ... ... „	5 45	6 5	6 45	7 5	8 5	9 5	10 5	11 0	...
Poole Library ... ... „	5 50	6 10	6 50	7 10	8 10	9 10	10 10	10 10	11 5	...
Hamilton Road (Lake Road) arr	6 0	6 20	7 0	7 20	8 20	9 20	10 20	...

	NSu	NSu	NSu	NSu	NSu	NSu	Su	NSu		NSu		NSu		NSu		NSu		NSu
Hamilton Road (Lake Road) dep	7 15	BX	...	8 10	8 35	9 10	9 30	...	10 10	10 30	11 10	11 30	12 10	12 30	1 10	1 30	2 10	2 30	3 10	3 30	4 10
Poole Library ... ... „	7 25	7 30	7 55	8 20	8 45	9 20	9 40	9 45	10 20	10 40	11 20	11 40	12 20	12 40	1 20	1 40	2 20	2 40	3 20	3 40	4 20
Stanley Green ... ... „	7 30	7 35	8 0	8 25	8 50	9 25	9 45	9 50	10 25	10 45	11 25	11 45	12 25	1 25	1 45	2 25	2 45	3 25	3 45	4 25
Oakdale School ... ... „	7 31	7 36	8 1	8 26	8 51	9 26	9 46	9 51	10 26	10 46	11 26	11 46	12 26	1 26	1 46	2 26	2 46	3 26	3 46	4 26
Foxholes (Housing Estate) arr	7 35	7 C40	8 5	8 30	8 55	9 30	9 50	9 55	10 30	10 50	11 30	11 50	12 30	12 50	1 30	1 50	2 30	2 50	3 30	3 50	4 30

	NSu		NSu		NSu			
Hamilton Road (Lake Road) dep	4 30	5 10	5 30	6 10	6 30	7 5	7 30	8 30	9 30	10 30	...
Poole Library ... ... „	4 40	5 20	5 40	6 20	6 40	7 15	7 40	8 40	9 40	10 40	...
Stanley Green ... ... „	4 45	5 25	5 45	6 25	6 45	...	7 45	8 45	9 45	10 45	...
Oakdale School ... ... „	4 46	5 26	5 46	6 26	6 46	...	7 46	8 46	9 46	10 46	...
Foxholes (Housing Estate) arr	4 50	5 30	5 50	6 30	6 50	...	7 50	8 50	9 50	10 50	...

NSu—Not Sundays.   Su—Sundays only.   BX—Runs to Bear Cross.   C—Time at Cemetery Junction.

1952

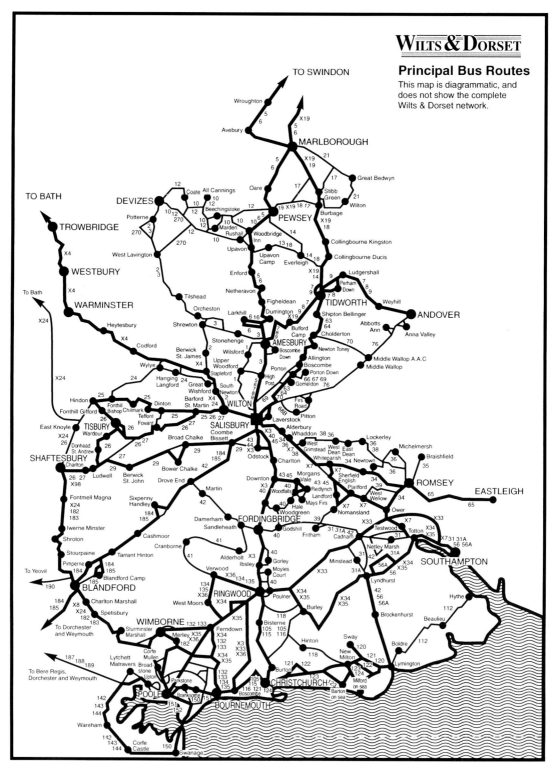

WILTS & DORSET

Principal Bus Routes

This map is diagrammatic, and does not show the complete Wilts & Dorset network.

1999

EXPLORING

WILTS & DORSET

COUNTRY

· A PAST AND PRESENT COMPANION ·

Chris Harris

·TOWN AND COUNTRY HERITAGE·
from
The NOSTALGIA *Collection*

First published in 2000
Reprinted 2002

British Library Cataloguing in Publication Data

A catalogue record for this book is available from the British Library.

ISBN 1 85895 176 3

Past & Present Publishing Ltd
The Trundle
Ringstead Road
Great Addington
Kettering
Northants
NN14 4BW

Tel/Fax: 01536 330588
email: sales@nostalgiacollection.com
Website: www.nostalgiacollection.com

Printed and bound in Great Britain

Past and
Present

A Past & Present book
from
The NOSTALGIA *Collection*

Acknowledgements

While we were walking in the Purbeck Hills one day in February 1999, my good friend Marion Hawker suddenly said to me, 'You should write a book!' Having thought about this, I contacted Past & Present Publishing, and have been honoured to accept their invitation to write *Exploring Wilts & Dorset Country Past and Present*.

I would like to thank Dave and Betty Underwood of Classic Pictures in Christchurch for permission to reproduce pictures from their stock; Andrew Bryce, Operations Director of Wilts & Dorset Bus Company, for allowing me to use photographs from the company's collection; Rev Jonathan Foster, Vicar of the Parish of Branksome St Clement, and Tom Reiblein for the photographs on page 17.

Thanks also to Christchurch Borough Council for the photograph of a Wilts & Dorset bus outside their Town Hall in 1953; to Richard Weaver, Chris Allnatt and Ray Humphries for their photographs; to Rachel Hawker for taking the photograph of me refuelling my car; and to Lisa Connell for lending me the photograph on page 95. I am also grateful to Vin Almond of Pindar, Preston, for his help with the map.

Many people have provided information, and I would especially thank Heather Raggett of Kinson Library and Paula Brooks of the Cherry Tree Montessori School, Ashley Heath.

Finally, a special word of thanks to my Mother, who years ago had said that I should write a book, for her great interest and her words of support and encouragement each time I have visited her.

Contents

1952

These photographs date from the early 1950s and show the interior of Bournemouth Bus Station before the rebuilding of 1957-8. The 1930s Art Deco style is very apparent: note especially the window above the pedestrian exit from the bus departure bays to Exeter Road. Of interest in the waiting room is the large route map – divided into Western and Eastern sections, which are separated by the stairs leading down to the Royal Blue Coach Station below. The shaped wooden panels at cornice level in the waiting room depict the history of transport through the ages. They were removed in 1957 when the building was modernised, but fortunately they were not thrown away, and the author now has them in his office! For more information about Bournemouth Bus Station, together with 'past and present' photographs, see pages 25-27. *Both Wilts & Dorset collection*

Introduction

Have you ever visited somewhere, looked at a view, street scene or building and thought, 'I wonder how that looked in days gone by?' Or perhaps you can recall former landmarks that no longer exist, like the Amity Cinema in Poole or some of the delightful branch-line railway stations that were closed during the Beeching era in the 1960s. Then I hope you will like this book. In it we take a nostalgic journey through some of the places served by the Wilts & Dorset Bus Company. We start from Poole and travel through Bournemouth, Christchurch, Highcliffe and New Milton to Lymington and the New Forest, then continue northwards through Ringwood and the Avon Valley to Salisbury and Wiltshire before returning to Dorset and finishing our journey in Swanage, having made a circular tour around the company's operating area.

Photographs taken from the 1900s to the 1960s are paired with modern photographs of the same location; it is fascinating to see how some places have changed very little in almost 100 years, while in other instances the view is barely recognisable after a period of less than 40 years.

In referring to the Wilts & Dorset area, I do of course mean the territory served by the present day Wilts & Dorset Bus Company, which came into existence in April 1983 when the then Hants & Dorset Motor Services was broken up into smaller units for privatisation. Many readers will know that the name Wilts & Dorset had previously been seen on the sides of buses running in the Salisbury area from 1915 until 1971, and had only disappeared as a consequence of having merged with Hants & Dorset in 1965.

In the final chapter we look at the development of road and rail transport from the 1930s to the 1990s. I am particularly pleased to include many previously unpublished interior views of various types of buses, coaches and railway carriages; after all, it was the interior that was of the greatest interest to the majority of the passengers. As far as the pre-1971 period is concerned, I have concentrated on the buses and coaches of the former Hants & Dorset company, partly because of the number of interesting photographs available, partly because the 'old' Wilts & Dorset has been very well served in Steve Chislett's excellent book (*Wilts & Dorset 1915-1995: 80 years of Motor Services*, published by Millstream Books), and perhaps mostly because I remember travelling and in some cases working on these buses.

Ever since childhood I have loved exploring. As a youngster I liked nothing better during the school holidays than to ride around on lowbridge Bristol Ks with a Day Out ticket (an on-bus-issued insert Setright and forerunner of today's Explorer or Getaway), or to search out some of the more bucolic corners of the local railway network with a Runabout Rover ticket – a whole week to travel about in comfortable Maunsell or Bulleid carriages for only 15 shillings (75p) if you were under 14! And in those easy-going days there were always friendly transport staff who were happy to chat and share their memories with a young lad who enjoyed solitary travel just for the sake of it. It was probably inevitable that in due course I too would join the transport industry, which I am pleased to say in the Wilts & Dorset area still retains its friendly image. I feel very privileged to have seen at first hand some of the changes illustrated in this book, either during my delightfully free-range childhood or during my very happy years with Hants & Dorset Motor Services and the Wilts & Dorset Bus Company. I have also derived great pleasure from researching the information to caption the earlier photographs.

I hope you will enjoy reading this book as much as I have enjoyed writing it.

Chris Harris
Poole, Dorset

Hants & Dorset coach No F564 (CEL 229) came into the fleet in May 1936. It is a Leyland Tiger TS7 carrying bodywork by Beadle with seating for 28 passengers giving very good comfort and leg room. This photograph was taken in 1937, showing the coach in Hants & Dorset's green and cream coach livery and marked up for an afternoon tour.

Poole

THE QUAY, POOLE.

E 02977

POOLE QUAY: When the 'past' photograph of Poole Quay was taken around 1912, the area was dominated by industry. The stone quayside seen here had replaced the previous wooden piles and platforms in 1909-10. Just in front of the old Poole Pottery kilns can be seen the fish shambles, demolished in 1914. In recent years a modern replica shambles has been erected, and is used as a shelter by people enjoying a stroll along the Quay, which, as the 1999 photograph shows, is now a popular leisure destination.

The gasworks' coal transporter is visible in the background of the 1912 photograph. In the days of coal gas, coal was unloaded from ships' holds and transported in tubs along the aerial ropeway across part of the town to the gasworks. This ceased only when the town was converted to natural gas, and the transporter was demolished in the early 1970s.

Note the railway lines along the Quay in the old photograph. This branch ran from a point beside the present Weymouth-bound platform at Poole Station along West Quay Road and on to the Quay itself. It opened in June 1874, and trucks 'parked' in the way seen beneath the coal transporter were a common sight until the line closed in May 1960. The tracks – a hazard for cyclists – were lifted in 1962.

Note how a number of the old warehouses have been converted for other uses, including Natural World at Hennings Wharf. However, the parked cars on the right of the 1999 photograph conceal one remaining feature from the 1912 photograph – the large metal ships' mooring bollards. *Classic Pictures/CH*

HIGH STREET, POOLE. '52

LOWER HIGH STREET: When these two photographs taken at the Poole Quay end of Poole High Street are compared with those on the following pages, which were taken further up the same street, it becomes even more remarkable how little this particular section has changed in the 50 or so years that separate the two photographs. In the left foreground the lower floor of the King's Head has been altered, while a different antelope now gives its name to the Antelope Hotel next door! All that has really altered about the building on the right is the removal of the dormer windows from the roof and a change in the tenancies of the shops.

Traffic can still use this part of the High Street, as shown by the number of parked cars in the July 1999 view; bicycles outnumber cars in the 1940s photograph, and note the tradesman's cart-horse enjoying his nosebag on the right! The High Street bends sharply to the south by what was then Hancock's and what is now a fast food outlet; the road proceeding straight on behind the photographer is Sarum Street. Traffic can no longer go this way, and the pavement has been modified as can be seen in the 1999 photograph. Of interest is the replica gas lamp standard in the 'present' view; this is of a type common on many Poole streets until they were replaced during the 1960s. They are now being replicated in this way in areas where a 'period' atmosphere is required.
Classic Pictures/CH

HIGH STREET AND AMITY HALL: A prominent landmark halfway along Poole High Street is the Midland Bank building, which has changed very little in the 85 years that separate these two photographs. Pedestrianisation of this part of the High Street allows people to wander down the road as they did in the early years of this century, and in a way that would have been unthinkable 30-40 years ago! It has also allowed the planting of trees, one of which, together with a large information board, now partly conceals the front of the bank.

The Amity Hall, on the left of the 1914 picture, was built in 1882 and by 1931 had become the Amity Cinema. This closed in 1959, and there were public protests when it was demolished to make way for the present Woolworths store, which moved from another site further along the street. While the buildings on the right-hand side of the photographs have changed little, much of the left side has been completely remodelled, although Hawkes shoe shop can be recognised in both pictures. Note again the replica street lamps in the 1999 view. *Classic Pictures/CH*

THE ANSTY ARMS stood on the corner of Poole High Street and Towngate Street. When Hall & Woodhouse opened this hostelry in the late 1860s their brewery, established by Charles Hall in 1777, was at Ansty in deepest Dorset. Their present brewery at Blandford St Mary was built in 1899. By the late 1940s, the date of the 'past' view, traffic was very heavy at this point, and it can be seen that the services of a policeman on point duty were needed.

Most of the buildings shown in the old photograph were demolished in 1984, and the area has now been completely pedestrianised, this being made possible by the opening of the Towngate Bridge in 1971. The area is now known as Falkland Square, after the South Atlantic conflict of the early 1980s in which the Poole-based Royal Marines were involved. One feature can be recognised in the distance in both photographs: the unusual corner tower on the roof of what in the 1940s was Butler's furniture store, but which in 1999 was a Burger King restaurant! *Classic Pictures/CH*

REGENT CINEMA: Looking at this picture of Poole's Regent Cinema, taken in the late 1940s, it is hard to believe that the 1999 photograph was taken in the same place, as absolutely nothing remains from the earlier view. The cinema was built in 1926, and in 1931 a fine Christie organ, voiced for the building, was installed there. The Regent closed as a cinema in the summer of 1968, but continued to be used for bingo until 1977. The organ was removed in 1968 and set up in the Antelope Hotel at the other end of the High Street (see page 10), but in 1974 was moved again to Sandford Park near Wareham. After the Regent ceased to be used for bingo in 1977 the building was soon demolished together with the nearby shops and the Port Mahon Castle public house to make way for stage two of the Arndale (now Dolphin) shopping centre, opened in 1979. Today's shoppers can stand and chat where traffic once travelled along the upper High Street. *Classic Pictures/CH*

HIGH St. POOLE.

UPPER HIGH STREET: Not a single building visible in the 1961 photograph of the upper end of Poole High Street remains standing in 1999. The first roundabout at the junction with Wimborne Road was built in 1962; it was extended in 1967 when Kingland Road was transferred to its present alignment, and again in 1971 with the opening of Towngate Bridge. All of the buildings on the left of the 1961 photograph had been demolished by late 1967 to make way for the first stage of the Arndale Centre development, which opened to shoppers in 1969. The most visible part of this in the 1999 photograph is the Central Library; this opened in May 1970 and uses part of the Centre originally intended as a dance hall.

The construction of the second stage of the Arndale Centre in 1979 completely closed the High Street at this point; this development is almost completely hidden by the now mature trees on the roundabout. Note the Mini among the parked cars in the 1961 photograph, and also the rather unusual street lamp in the left foreground, which is mounted on a pole previously used to support electric cables for trams. Most of the tramway poles continued in use as street lights after trams ceased to run in 1935; they were gradually replaced, but a few remained into the 1970s. *Classic Pictures/CH*

POOLE HOSPITAL: In 1897 the Poole Mansion House in Market Street, which had been built for Sir Peter Thompson in 1751, was given by Lord & Lady Wimborne for use as a hospital. It was opened as the Cornelia Hospital, named after Lady Wimborne. This soon became too small and a new purpose-built hospital was opened in Longfleet Road in 1907. Still called the Cornelia Hospital, it is seen in the 'past' picture when newly built. Following the passing of the National Health Service Act, 1946, its title was changed to Poole General Hospital, and in recent times it has become simply Poole Hospital.

In the years following the Second World War the expanding population of the Poole area put increased pressure on the hospital accommodation, and in the 1950s authorisation was given for the building, in stages, of a large new hospital. This was completed in 1969 and formally opened by Her Majesty the Queen on 11 July of that year. The modern photograph, taken in May 1999, shows the contrast in the buildings, with the spire of St Mary's Church in the background fixing the location. *Classic Pictures/CH*

Sea View Rd & Poole Rd, Newtown.

NEWTOWN: It is largely the contours of the ground, plus some of the buildings in the background, that confirm that these two photographs were taken from the same point. When the 'past' photograph was taken in around 1900, both Sea View Road and Ringwood Road (then called Poole Road) were still gravel surfaced. The large building in the centre of the 1900 photograph was for many years Newtown Post Office, but around 1964 it was transferred to occupy one side of a grocery store (Hardiman's), which at that time was located in one of the shops in the row seen on the right of the 1999 photograph. The rambling building of the former Post Office stood empty and derelict for a few years before being demolished in the late 1960s. The road junction was then remodelled with traffic lights in the form seen in the 1999 view.

In the 1980s the Post Office was moved again and is now in the parade of shops in Sea View Road seen on the left of the 'present' photograph. The row of shops in Ringwood Road (on the right) was built in the 1930s, and as recently as the 1960s consisted of a bakery, a barber, the grocery store already mentioned and a hardware store. By November 1999 only one business was trading from the row – a plumbing and heating supplies company, whose eye-catching advertising logo can be seen on the end of the block. *Classic Pictures/CH*

THE PARISH CHURCH OF BRANKSOME ST CLEMENT was built in 1889 on a site given by Mr William Pearce of Springfield House, Parkstone. The cost of construction, amounting to £3,000, was met by Lord Wimborne. As built the church consisted of a chancel, nave, south porch and vestry, but was planned so that a north aisle could be added at a later date, the north wall consisting of a row of arches with a brick-faced wall immediately beyond.

The first photograph shows the interior of the church in 1937, while the 1996 photograph was taken from the west gallery, added in 1974. Other changes are also apparent: the wooden pulpit was replaced around 1960 by that from the now demolished St Paul's Church in Poole High Street, and the north aisle was added and the

chancel re-ordered for the church's centenary in 1989, while during the 1990s modern lighting was fitted. The comfortable pews remain, as does the lectern, given by parishioners as a thanks offering for God's gifts of victory and peace after the 1914-18 war. The Bevington organ was originally installed in Canford Magna Church in 1878. It was placed in St Clement's Church during the 1930s, being rebuilt by E. C. Bishop & Sons in 1939. During 2000 a major rebuild by Lance Foy will see the organ resited on the west gallery. *St Clement's Parochial Church Council collection/Tom Reiblein*

THE REGAL CINEMA, PARKSTONE, on the corner of Ashley Road and Jubilee Road in Upper Parkstone, and seen here around 1962, was opened in September 1935. For over 25 years it was a very well used local cinema, attracting good audiences and with popular children's presentations on Saturday mornings. However, mass television ownership quickly meant that, in common with many cinemas at the time, the Regal was sadly no longer a commercial proposition. Closure came in October 1963, and following demolition the site was turned over to retail use.

The unit that is now the Iceland shop was opened as a Victor Value supermarket, and later became a Tesco 'Home & Wear' store, while the shop on the corner, which is now Coral's bookmakers, was originally H. C. Peal's gentlemen's outfitters. Boots the Chemist has moved a few doors down the road to the third of the new units. The roofline of the shops on the left of both photographs is unchanged, and although Currys has now become a Scope charity shop, Woolworths is still there, albeit with an updated corporate image. *Classic Pictures/CH*

7389, BROADWAY, PARKSTONE.

ASHLEY ROAD, UPPER PARKSTONE, has long been an important local shopping centre. Years ago that part of the road near its junctions with Madeira Road and Albert Road was known as Broadway. The building lines are well back from the road here, and after the gardens were removed and the whole width given over to public highway and pavements, what was literally a broad way was created. In 1999 the wall of the Abbey National Building Society on the corner of Madeira Road (left foreground) still carried a very old street name sign 'Broadway'. Trams ran along Ashley Road from April 1901 until June 1935; in the 1920s photograph we see a tram, working through from Poole to Christchurch, at the Albert Road stop.

The roof lines of the buildings on the left and in the right foreground are little changed, but the large building on the right, occupied by Superdrug in the 1999 view, was built in the 1960s as a Tesco supermarket. The junction with Madeira Road was closed to traffic in the 1970s, and in 1999 flower beds and seats occupy the former roadway. The large building just visible in the centre right background of the 1920s photograph is the Victory Palace Cinema on the corner of Jubilee Road. This was operational from 1920 until February 1935, when it was demolished and replaced by the Regal Cinema seen on the opposite page. *Classic Pictures/CH*

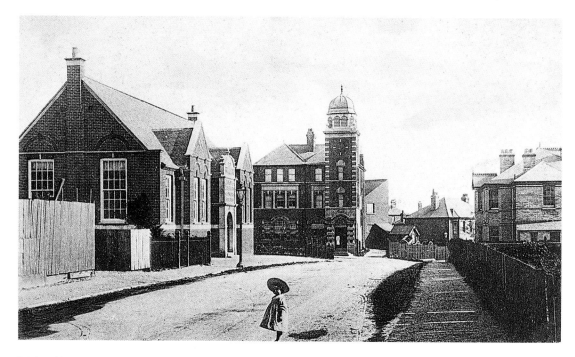

BRANKSOME LIBRARY: Until 1905 an area stretching from County Gates at Westbourne across to Newtown was administered by Branksome Urban District Council. The Council Buildings on the corner of Shillito Road were constructed in 1901, while the Library was given to Branksome UDC by the Scottish-born philanthropist Andrew Carnegie and opened in 1904. The 'past' view shows both buildings in 1905, the year that the area was amalgamated into the Borough of Poole. Over the years the former Branksome Council Buildings have been used for a variety of purposes, including a highway depot and a clinic. They have survived with very few external changes, and their presence can just be discerned through the large tree that dominates the centre of the November 1999 photograph. The house on the right of the photograph has lost its chimneys and attic rooms have been added, while an additional house has been built to the right of the Council Buildings.

Unfortunately the Library was virtually destroyed by fire on 16 March 1967 and had to be demolished, although within a fortnight improvised arrangements had been made to provide a small library in the old reading room. The replacement building seen here came into use on 23 April 1968. At the time of writing there are plans to move the Library to premises in the nearby main Ashley Road. *Classic Pictures/CH*

PARKSTONE STATION opened in June 1874, and was spacious and attractive, with a goods yard on the down side (ie behind the platform on the right of the photographs). Seen here around 1910, and for many years little changed, the roof of the footbridge was removed around 1960 and the goods yard closed in September 1966; however, in most respects the scene in the early 1970s would have altered little from that of 60 years earlier. The station was still lit by gas and the by then decaying structure was still clad in (peeling) Southern Railway green and light stone paint.

Modernisation came in the mid-1970s, when the buildings on the down platform were demolished and replaced by a simple shelter, while the extent of the canopy on the up platform was reduced, and electric lighting was installed. In 1986 the station was given Network SouthEast branding (which it still retains) and electrification of the line from Bournemouth to Weymouth from May 1988 has increased the number of trains calling at Parkstone. *Classic Pictures/CH*

CREEKMOOR HALT: The section of railway from Broadstone (then called New Poole Junction) to the present Poole Station opened in December 1872. However, Creekmoor Halt was not opened until 19 June 1933. Construction was of typical Southern Railway design, with pre-cast concrete being much in evidence. The 'past' picture dates from 1963 and shows British Railways Standard Class 4 tank engine No 80146 arriving with a train for Bournemouth West. A number of people can be seen waiting for the train – Creekmoor was very well used by local residents – but the line closed to passengers from 7 March 1966. The rails stayed down until 1977, being used by freight trains to and from West Moors.

After complete closure the trackbed was used for the construction of the Broadstone Relief Road, and a comparison of the two photographs shows the road following the same line as the original railway. In the days of the railway there was a boarded foot crossing (visible in the 1963 photograph) from Creekmoor Lane to York Road. When the new road was built this facility was retained, with a pelican crossing at the same point. In addition, a bus link was provided, with bus-activated traffic signals, to allow buses to serve both the Creekmoor and Waterloo areas during the evening and on Sundays without opening up a short-cut for motorists to use as a 'rat run'. *Classic Pictures/CH*

Bournemouth

BOURNEMOUTH WEST STATION opened in June 1874 and was considerably enlarged in 1888, when the building shown in the 'past' picture was completed. This six-platform station was rather unusual for a terminus in that the main buildings were beside platform 4 rather than across the end of the tracks. Bournemouth West was the terminus for trains from the Somerset & Dorset line, from Salisbury and from Brockenhurst via West Moors, as well as for the Bournemouth portions of trains from London Waterloo, and had a special atmosphere of its own.

Closure came in 1965 as part of the project to electrify the London-Bournemouth line; it was necessary to construct a servicing area for the new electric trains across the running lines, which made it impractical to keep the station open. In any case by that time the closure of the lines to Salisbury and Brockenhurst via West Moors and the impending closure of the Somerset & Dorset line also made the economic grounds for the retention of Bournemouth West somewhat dubious. Nonetheless many people were sad when this popular station closed. The buildings, which had remained little changed from their condition in this 1910 view, were demolished in the spring of 1970; a coach park now stands on the site, and behind the coaches runs the Wessex Way town centre bypass. On the other side of the old station forecourt the appearance of the Queen's Hall Hotel has changed very little in the almost 90 years that separate the two photographs, and proves that they were both taken from the same location. *Classic Pictures/CH*

THE TRIANGLE, BOURNEMOUTH.

BOURNEMOUTH TRIANGLE was laid out and built in the mid-19th century, and at the time of the 'past' photograph, taken in around 1900, was a pleasant and genteel shopping area.

For many years the Triangle has been a terminus and layover point for Bournemouth's Yellow Buses, and, following the fire at Bournemouth Bus Station in July 1976, most Hants & Dorset buses running to and from Bournemouth also terminated here. In 1999 the Triangle is still the terminus for some Yellow Bus routes as well as for Wilts & Dorset services running north and east from Bournemouth. Wilts & Dorset have a Travel Office at number 27, part of the premises occupied by T. Rogers almost 100 years earlier. Notice how the original window design has survived on this shop.

There have been considerable alterations to the shop fronts on the rest of the buildings, and at some time the roof balustrade has been lost, but the area is still easily recognisable. The buildings on the south of the Triangle are in a poor state and some of the shops are boarded up in the 1999 photograph. The area to the left of Avenue Lane is obscured by a tree in this view, but the buildings formerly here were acquired by a developer and demolished in the early 1980s. This was in preparation for the first stage of a new shopping precinct intended to revitalise the area, but despite a number of schemes being proposed over the years nothing has been built and the land has been used as a car park. At the time of writing there are plans to build a new Bournemouth Central Library on the site. *Classic Pictures/CH*

BOURNEMOUTH BUS STATION: By the late 1920s the number of buses and coaches terminating at Bournemouth Square was starting to cause problems in terms of lack of available roadside standing space. To overcome this, a combined bus and coach station was built in nearby Exeter Road, with Hants & Dorset buses using the upper level while Royal Blue had a coach station beneath. Bournemouth Bus and Coach Station was opened in March 1931, as seen in the first view, and in 1937 further land to the rear was acquired and surfaced to provide additional bus departure stands.

In March 1957 work started to enlarge and modernise the premises, and two extra floors above the original building became Hants & Dorset's Head Office in September 1958, as shown in the second photograph, dating from October 1957.

A huge fire in the early hours of Sunday 25 July 1976 caused such damage that the building eventually had to be demolished; in 1999 the site is used as a car park, while Exeter Road has been realigned as part of a town centre improvement scheme. *Classic Pictures/Wilts & Dorset collection/ CH*

THE NEW OMNIBUS AND COACH STATION, BOURNEMOUTH

BOURNEMOUTH BUS STATION is seen again on the left in October 1957 and November 1999; the church fixes the location of the northward-looking photographs. Notice the bus stands at the rear of the building in the 1957 view, again showing it in course of enlargement, while the realignment and higher level of Exeter Road can be seen in the 1999 picture.

The photographs on this page are looking across towards Exeter Crescent, and illustrate how the car park takes up the land previously used by the buses and coaches. There are photographs showing the interior of the Bus Station in the early 1950s on page 6. *Wilts & Dorset collection (2)/CH (2)*

76   BOURNEMOUTH – Old Christchurch Road. — LL.

BEALE'S DEPARTMENT STORE: John Elmes Beale, who had formerly been a draper's assistant, opened a shop in Hinton Road, Bournemouth, in the early 1880s. The business soon expanded, taking over adjacent shops and in due course becoming a major department store. By the time of the 'past' photograph, taken in 1912, Beale's Fancy Fair had a commanding position on the corner of Hinton Road and Old Christchurch Road, and was one of Bournemouth's best-known shops. An extensive refurbishment in the art deco style fashionable at the time transformed the appearance of the building from 1931, but during the Second World War the store was completely destroyed by a direct hit during an air raid at lunchtime on Sunday 23 May 1943.

After the war the store was rebuilt in the then contemporary style, and is seen here in July 1999. Beale's remains in the ownership of the same family, and is still one of Bournemouth's top stores. In addition there are new Beale's stores in Poole, Winchester, Walton-on-Thames, Bedford, Kendal, Southport (trading as Broadbents & Boothroyds), Bolton (trading as Whitakers) and Yeovil (trading as Denners). *Classic Pictures/CH*

KINSON: While a number of features can be recognised in both of these views of Kinson, there have also been many changes in the almost 50 years that separate the two photographs. The building on the right of the 'past' photograph is the old Kinson School, dating from 1836 and enlarged in 1890 and 1927. The premises were still too small, however, and the school moved to its present site in School Lane in September 1936. Part of the old school building was then used for the first Kinson Library, which opened on 1 August 1940 with a stock of 3,000 books. By all accounts conditions in the still gas-lit building were far from ideal, and the library was moved to a prefabricated building in July 1949. This in turn was replaced by the present Kinson Library, which opened in June 1970. Meanwhile the old school had continued to be used by the Sunday School and the Boys' Brigade, but was demolished in the late 1950s.

The buildings in the left foreground are quite recognisable, although more of them have now had their ground floors converted into shops. The public house in the middle distance has also changed little, but is now called Gulliver's Tavern (rather than The Dolphin) in memory of a locally famous smuggler. The Yellow Bus in the 'past' picture is a 1950 Leyland Titan PD 2/3 with Weymann bodywork; its counterpart in the modern view is a 1999 Dennis Trident with East Lancs bodywork. *Classic Pictures/CH*

BEAR CROSS: The original inn at Bear Cross was a thatched cottage built a little to the rear of the site of the modern Bear Cross Hotel. The hostelry was well placed at the crossroads of two important thoroughfares, although at the time of the 'past' photograph these were narrow tree-lined lanes with grass verges.

The present Bear Cross Hotel was built in 1931 in front of the original thatched building, which was pulled down after the new premises opened. The first landlord of the new hotel was Philip Mead, a well-known cricketer who played for England in 19 tests. Bear Cross in 1999 is still a busy junction, and a roundabout new dominates the picture. The area has seen considerable development in the years following the end of the Second World War, and the modern view is a far cry from the tranquil scene photographed around 90 years earlier. *Classic Pictures/CH*

174. Pier Approach, Bournemouth.

BOURNEMOUTH PIER APPROACH: There are comparatively few people in our 'past' photograph of Bournemouth Pier Approach taken around 1922. Notice Sydenham's fancy goods, stationery and book shop with the public baths behind. These buildings were replaced by larger swimming baths in 1937, but those too have now been demolished. In their place the new IMAX cinema development is seen nearing completion in the 'present' photograph taken on 29 August 1999. The pathway to East Cliff beside the building remains, and can be seen in both photographs.

A flyover built during the 1970s keeps the Pier Approach area free of traffic, and various funfair attractions have been provided for the summer crowds. The pier entrance buildings have been completely rebuilt and considerably extended, while in the right foreground can be seen part of the roof of the new Oceanarium. In the background blocks of flats dominate the 1999 scene. *Classic Pictures/CH*

BOSCOMBE PIER was opened on 29 July 1889 by the Duke of Argyll; it was 600 feet long and built of iron. Promoted by the Boscombe Pier Company, roller-skating and musical entertainments were listed among its attractions. The pier was taken over by Bournemouth Corporation in 1903, and the 'past' photograph shows a paddle-steamer arriving, probably around 1912.

Some reconstruction work was done on the pier in 1925, but, like Bournemouth Pier, it was breached as an anti-invasion measure in 1940. Rebuilt in its present form in 1957-8 using concrete, the rather functional 1950s design seen in the 'present' picture can be contrasted with the more ornate earlier structure. Unfortunately today Boscombe Pier is in a very run-down condition. The 'Mermaid' pavilion at the pierhead is closed, and the area beside and beyond it is fenced off – this is just visible in the photograph. Notices warn those taking a stroll that the pier beyond that point is 'considered unsafe'. *Classic Pictures/CH*

POKESDOWN STATION was opened in July 1886. In its original form, as seen in the 'past' photograph dating from 1901, the station had a relatively small entrance from the road, with stairs leading down to a central island platform. In 1931 the station was rebuilt by the Southern Railway in what was then its latest style, with separate up and down platforms on the outer sides of the newly quadrupled tracks (reduced again to two in 1972). The basic structure remains little changed from that time, but was given Network SouthEast branding in 1986, which is now out of date.

The New Era Laundry, formerly on the corner of Clarence Park Road, has been demolished in recent years and replaced by the modern houses seen in the 1999 photograph. Motor cars have replaced the horse and cart, and the needs of motorists are catered for by the filling station just visible beyond the houses. *Classic Pictures/CH*

Christchurch and Highcliffe area

CHRISTCHURCH HIGH STREET: The Old Town Hall in Christchurch High Street was built in 1859 and extended with additional offices at the rear during the 1890s. In the 'past' photograph we see the Town Hall in 1953, decorated for the Coronation. The Wilts & Dorset bus, HHR 822, is a Bristol KSW5G with Eastern Coach Works lowbridge bodywork (see page 80) working from Bournemouth to Salisbury on service 38, which was operated jointly with Hants & Dorset. In 1960 there were plans to demolish the Town Hall along with other buildings on the east side of the High Street to allow for road widening, but these proposals were subsequently abandoned.

The offices of Christchurch Borough Council moved to a new building in Bridge Street in 1980. The buildings at the rear of the Old Town Hall were demolished during 1981 and the area developed as the Saxon Square shopping precinct, which opened in April 1983. The photograph taken in May 1994 shows the Old Town Hall, now the Mayor's Parlour, at the entrance to Saxon Square. This photograph is taken from a slightly different angle in order to show other changes, including the extended pedestrian area in front of the building complete with clock, the repositioning of the bus stops and the demolition and replacement of the buildings to the north of the

Mayor's Parlour on the east side of the High Street. A Wilts & Dorset 31-seat Optare single-deck bus is on service 123 bound for Lymington, with a sister bus of the same type in the background waiting to depart for Ringwood via Bransgore and Burley. *Christchurch Borough Council/Wilts & Dorset collection*

HURN STATION, on the line from Ringwood to Christchurch, opened in November 1862. However, after the opening of the direct route from Brockenhurst to Christchurch via Sway in 1888, the line via Hurn became a quiet backwater. By 1929 Hurn station was issuing an average of only seven tickets per day, and unsurprisingly the line from Ringwood to Christchurch closed in September 1935.

The buildings, however, have remained, now being used as the Avon Causeway Hotel, and in recent years have been considerably extended. A Pullman carriage, built in 1960 and withdrawn after a very short life on British Railways, stands close to the position occupied by the push-pull train in the earlier 1930s photograph.

The third view, taken from the forecourt, shows that in 1999 the building has retained its railway character to a remarkable extent, considering that it has not been used as a station for 64 years.
Classic Pictures/CH (2)

BURTON GREEN: The caption of this 1918 photograph describes Burton as being in Hampshire, which at that time indeed it was, being transferred to Dorset in the boundary changes of 1974. The building in the right foreground of both photographs is Burton Green House, and apart from alterations to the porch and downstairs windows its appearance in 1999 is very similar to that of 1918. Beyond can be seen the roof of St Luke's Church. This was designed by Benjamin Ferrey and built in 1874 at a cost of £3,500. In the 1999 photograph a road has been cut across the south side of the green; note also the increase in the size and number of trees. *Classic Pictures/CH*

HIGHCLIFFE CASTLE was built between 1830 and 1835 for Lord Stuart de Rothesay, who had been the Duke of Wellington's administrator during the Napoleonic Wars. It remained in the ownership of the same family until it was sold in 1950. For a short while it became a children's convalescent home, but in 1955 it was bought by the Claretian Fathers for use as a seminary. The Claretian Fathers left in 1967, and later that year the Great Hall was damaged by fire. A second fire in 1968 severely damaged the building, and for years the Castle remained empty and open to further damage by vandals and by the elements.

The Castle is now owned by Christchurch Borough Council who together with English Heritage have undertaken a programme of restoration. The grounds are now open to the public, as is part of the restored Castle, used as a visitor centre. A comparison of the 'past' and 'present' photographs gives little indication of the events of the intervening 50 years... *Classic Pictures/CH*

SEA CORNER, HIGHCLIFFE: In the mid-1930s there was very little traffic in Highcliffe and pedestrians could cross the road at Sea Corner without difficulty, but in 1999 traffic lights and a pelican crossing are needed at this busy junction. Misselbrook & Weston's shop on the corner of Gordon Road incorporated a rather ornate clock tower, added to commemorate the Coronation of King George V (see also page 41), the cost being met by local residents.

In the July 1999 photograph this shop has been rebuilt to become G&T's Original Warehouse, and the clock tower has been replaced by a rather functional fitment. Comparatively few changes have been made to the other four shops in the parade, but notice how the chimneys at the near end have been shortened and roofed over.
Classic Pictures/CH

New Milton, Lymington and the New Forest

OLD MILTON: These photographs compare the A337 road at Old Milton in the 1940s and 1999. The location can easily be recognised, and most of the changes have been evolutionary rather than revolutionary. The small postbox mounted in a brick pillar on the right has been replaced by the freestanding metal type more common in urban areas, while the shop, which is now the Post Office, has been extended.

The white-painted Wheatsheaf public house can be seen in the centre background of both photographs, and behind it is an end-on view of the George Inn. The George had been a public house since 1880, but closed in the autumn of 1999. Plans have been submitted for new development at Old Milton Green (opposite the George), and since this is a conservation area it is possible that the George will be retained and restored either as an inn or for a different use. At the time of writing no decision on this or the possible development of Old Milton Green had been taken; it will be interesting to compare the 1999 photograph with the scene, say, ten years later... *Classic Pictures/CH*

NEW MILTON STATION opened with the direct line from Brockenhurst to Christchurch in March 1888. However, the station house on the up side has the date 1886 above the front door, so it is likely that the buildings were completed two years before the line was opened. A Dutch-gable design was used for the main buildings on the up side, while a substantial wood-built structure was provided on the down side.

Comparing the photographs, it is pleasing to see that very little has changed; most of the buildings visible in the earlier photograph, which dates from around 1920, survive in the July 1999 view. Electric lighting has been installed, while the siding behind the down platform just visible in the 'past' photograph was removed after the goods yard closed at the end of 1966. The station has been served by third-rail electric trains since July 1967. The building in the background of both photographs is not a castle – simply a water tower given this ornate and attractive design. *Classic Pictures/CH*

PENNINGTON became a Parish in its own right in 1839; prior to that it had been included as part of Milford. These photographs, dating from the early 1930s and 1999, show the area known as The Square. The large building on the corner of Wainsford Road was Pennington School. This opened in September 1852 and is surely Victorian architecture at its best – note in particular the delightful bell tower. The clock was added to mark the Coronation of King George V (see also page 38). The school building survives today almost unaltered visually, but sadly it has ceased to be used for educational purposes in recent years, and is now occupied by a firm of auctioneers and valuers.

The Sportsmans Arms public house on the left also survives with few changes to its appearance. Gas street lighting has been replaced by electricity, and note how modern technology has enabled the telegraph poles to be simplified! *Classic Pictures/CH*

QUAY HILL, LYMINGTON: The history of Lymington dates back many centuries; acting as a trading centre for the Celts of the Iron Age, the area was conquered by the Jutes and Saxons, and in Norman times was acquired by the Duke of Devonshire, who granted the town a charter in around 1200. In the past, and notably during the 18th century, the major industry of the area was the refining of salt taken from the sea. In addition, Lymington was a thriving boat-building and shipping centre, and in due course many fine Georgian and Victorian buildings were constructed.

The traffic-free cobbled Quay Hill is a fine example of a street built at this time. The two photographs compare Quay Hill in around 1910 and 1999. Some of the windows of the buildings on the left have been modified, and a large tree now overhangs the right foreground, but in general the scene is readily recognisable after almost 90 years. The 1999 photograph was taken at lunchtime on Saturday 24 July, a beautiful summer day; compare the casual dress of the passers-by with the more formal attire of those walking on the hill in the earlier view. *Classic Pictures/CH*

LYMINGTON PIER STATION: Although the railway reached Lymington Town in 1858, it was not extended across the Lymington River to Lymington Pier until 1884, during which year the London & South Western Railway acquired the ferry route between Lymington and Yarmouth on the Isle of Wight. In the 'past' photograph, taken in around 1930, we see the then paddle-driven ferry beside the original station.

With the introduction of an end-loading car ferry in 1938, a slipway was constructed and the station was rebuilt with the platform extended northwards towards the camera; both foot passengers and vehicles joined the ferry via the slipway. The signal box seen in the past photograph was replaced in 1956 by a modern building further north and out of these photographs; this 1956 structure closed in 1968 but survives in 1999, albeit no longer in railway use. The line was electrified in 1967.

Following the arrival of the present ferry vessels *Cenred*, *Cenwulf* and *Caedman*, built in 1973, a new ferry terminal to the south of the station was opened in 1976. Subsequently the platform canopy has been demolished, and passengers now leave the platform at the south end and join the ferry by means of a link span. The 'present' photograph taken in July 1999 shows the rationalised facilities remaining at Lymington Pier; the ferry can just be seen at the far end of the platform, while in the centre and right foreground it is just possible to discern the remains of the 1938 slipway. *Classic Pictures/CH*

BROCKENHURST STATION opened on 1 June 1847 and was on the route from Southampton to Dorchester via Ringwood. The branch line to Lymington opened in July 1858, but the present main line via Sway to Christchurch was not opened until March 1888. The 'past' photograph, taken in the 1920s, shows the island platform on the up side and the down through platform and a down bay platform on the right.

The station was rebuilt by the Southern Railway in 1936. The down bay was converted into a loop, thus giving the station two island platforms; the up platform was also extended. A new canopy was provided on the down platform while an extension in the contemporary style was provided for the canopy on the up platform. The line to Ringwood and Wimborne closed in May 1964, but the main line and the branch to Lymington were electrified in July 1967. In common with many other stations, the goods yard, seen on the left of the 1920s photograph, is now a car park. *Classic Pictures/CH*

44

BEAULIEU VILLAGE: The name, pronounced 'Bewley' and meaning 'beautiful place', was given to this location by the monks who came across from France in 1204 to establish an abbey here. In the centre background of both of these views of Beaulieu's village street can be seen the Palace House, once the Great Gatehouse of the Abbey, and now open to the public.

It is remarkable how little the scene has changed in almost a hundred years. Some of the vegetation has grown, but the exteriors of the houses and shops show hardly any change – there is absolutely no difficulty in recognising the location. There is, however, one big difference; in the picture taken around 1900 just one horse is visible, but the view taken during the summer of 1999 shows the village street lined with parked cars. But it could be said that the motor car has played a large part in the recent history of Beaulieu. In the 1950s Lord Montagu opened a Motor Museum in the grounds of the Palace House, which developed and expanded and in 1972 became the National Motor Museum. Together with the other attractions in the area, the museum brings many thousands of visitors to Beaulieu each year. *Classic Pictures/CH*

MINSTEAD, situated about 3 miles north-west of Lyndhurst, is one of the most interesting New Forest villages. Its church is one of only two in the Forest mentioned in the Domesday Book and is of a unique design, while the churchyard contains the grave of Sir Arthur Conan Doyle. When the 'past' photograph of the village street, taken in the 1940s, is compared with the 'present' view, taken in July 1999, the scene can be recognised despite a number of changes that have taken place during the intervening 50 or so years. The thatched cottages seen centre right survive, although their outbuildings have been rationalised. Just visible behind them is the roof of Ye Olde Trusty Servante Inn, prominently advertised in the 1940s photograph, and still a popular hostelry in the 1990s. Note the traditional farm cart, seen out of use and upended in the 1940s view – a once commonplace country sight now long gone!

Rather more changes have taken place on the left-hand side of the road, but the building in the foreground survives, now surrounded by vegetation. A new fingerpost for the road junction now directs the way to more local places than its predecessor. Cattle and ponies still wander freely, although none are visible in the 'present' photograph. *Classic Pictures/CH*

BARTLEY POST OFFICE: The village of Bartley lies between Cadnam and Totton on the eastern fringe of the New Forest. In the days when the BBC Home Service (now Radio 4) was broadcast on medium wave, a local transmitter serving South Hampshire and South Wiltshire was sited at Bartley, broadcasting the West of England regional service on 206 metres; Dorset received the same programmes from Start Point on 285 metres.

The view looking northwards along Brockishill Road to the Post Office on the corner of New Inn Road and Chinham Road has changed little in the almost 80 years that separate the two photographs. The main alteration to the shop is that the entrance has been moved round into New Inn Road, but pleasingly the establishment remains as Bartley's Post Office. New railings have at some time been provided in Brockishill Road, while the trees on the left have grown considerably. In the 'present' photograph taken on Sunday 14 November 1999 10-year-old Tim Foster stands in the same spot as the youngsters seen in the earlier view, and illustrates how fashions for young people have changed over the years. *Classic Pictures/CH*

CROWN HOTEL, LYNDHURST: Almost 100 years separate these photographs of the Crown Hotel at Lyndhurst, but the location is easily recognisable in both views. Beyond stripping the climbing plants from the walls, very few external changes have been made to the Crown Hotel or the other visible buildings.

The big change is, of course, the traffic. No way could the girls pose with their bicycles in the middle of the road in 1999! The traffic direction sign is interesting – do many people making for Southampton go as directed via the A337, M27 and M271, which is rather longer than the old route via the A35? Perhaps this is an illustration of the old country saying: 'Signposts be for strangers and not for them that know'! Just to the right of the photographs is the churchyard where Alice Liddell, the real-life girl on whom Lewis Carroll based the 'Alice in Wonderland' stories, is buried. *Classic Pictures/CH*

HIGH STREET, LYNDHURST: Lyndhurst is regarded as the 'capital' of the New Forest, and is the home of the New Forest District Council (at Appletree Court) and the New Forest Verderers (at Queen's House). As with the views of the Crown Hotel opposite, it is easy to recognise the buildings in these two photographs. The shop fronts on the left have been modernised, but the buildings remain in retail use, and there have been few external changes to the Stag Hotel on the right.

When the 'past' photograph was taken in the early 1930s, Lyndhurst High Street was open to two-way traffic. This section of road has now been one way (eastbound) for many years, and in the modern photograph, taken during the early evening of Thursday 1 July 1999, cones and blocks can be seen marking out a temporary traffic control measure. *Classic Pictures/CH*

BURLEY, situated in the west of the New Forest, is a classic 'picture postcard'-type village, visited by many tourists each year. It is also a good starting point for forest walks. At a quick glance it appears that there have been relatively few changes in the 50 or so years that separate these two photographs. However, closer inspection reveals a significant difference in that whereas the shops and businesses seen in the 1940s photograph were catering mainly for the needs of local residents, in 1999 most of the establishments were aiming their wares at the tourist trade.

Lloyds Bank has closed, but the former design of the shopfront can still be seen when looking at the Witchcraft shop that now occupies the building, and the old bracket for the bank sign still remains. The former 'Garage and Motor Works' is now the Odd Spot Gallery, and two of the shops seen in the background are also primarily concerned with selling items of interest to visitors. However, the Post Office at the right-hand end of the row remains. Notice how the yellow lines keep the village free of parked cars in the 1999 photograph. *Classic Pictures/CH*

BURLEY: These photographs were taken from a position slightly to the south of those opposite, and we are now looking in the other direction; the garage and the Lloyds Bank sign provide points of reference.

Notice how the garage has been altered in the few years that separate this 1950s photograph from the earlier view opposite; its modernised appearance can still be recognised in its 1999 role as the Odd Spot Gallery. The Burley Stores remains as a local shop in 1999; the pedestrianised Mall beside it leads to a car park, which has replaced the on-street parking of earlier years. The Esso petrol pumps seen on the left of the 1950s photograph have gone, replaced by the Coach House Tea Rooms. The thatched building in the centre background of both photographs is the Manor Farm Tea Room, which is virtually unchanged. Again, it is a refreshing contrast that fewer cars can be seen in the 1999 photograph than in the older view. *Classic Pictures/CH*

HOLMSLEY STATION opened on 1 June 1847, and was known as Christchurch Road until a station was opened in Christchurch in 1862. The nearest village was Burley, about 2 miles to the north. Thus for most of its life the station was very quiet, its busiest period probably being between 1942 and 1946 when considerable traffic was handled to and from the nearby wartime Holmsley Aerodrome. However, by 1963, when we see a BR Standard Class 3 tank engine with two Maunsell carriages (see page 92) entering the station with a Brockenhurst to Bournemouth West train, an average of only seven tickets a day were issued at Holmsley. Unsurprisingly, the station was closed from 4 May 1964.

After closure some of the trackbed was sold to Hampshire County Council for use in a road improvement scheme to eliminate the dangerous crossroads at Wilverley Post; local traffic now follows the route of the former railway line under the A35 through the bridge that can be seen in both photographs. The main station building survives and, with some modern extensions, is now a delightful tea room.

The road signposted to Lyndhurst and Southampton cuts across the site of the old Bournemouth-bound platform, but in the forest behind the photographer some of it remains more or less intact. The third photograph shows 10-year-old Timothy Foster on 3 September 1999 wishing that he could have the experience of catching a steam train to Bournemouth West! *Classic Pictures/CH (2)*

Around Ringwood and the Avon valley

RINGWOOD STATION opened with the line from Southampton to Dorchester on 1 June 1847, then in November 1862 a branch was opened from Ringwood to Christchurch via Hurn (see page 35). The 'past' view shows the quite large station with its rather unusual footbridge in around 1920; the photograph was taken from the New Street level crossing looking towards Brockenhurst. The short siding on the left was removed in 1930, and in September 1935 the branch to Hurn and Christchurch was closed.

Ringwood station closed to passengers with the line from Brockenhurst to Broadstone on 4 May 1964, but remained open for freight, served from the Broadstone direction, until August 1967. The track was subsequently lifted, the buildings demolished, and a road has been built on this section of the old formation. A link with the past has been maintained by calling the road Castleman Way after the chief promoter of the railway line, but it has to be said that relatively few casual visitors to the area in 1999 would realise that 35 years earlier a railway station had stood at this point. *Classic Pictures/CH*

MARKET DAY, RINGWOOD.

RINGWOOD MARKET PLACE: The Wednesday Market at Ringwood has a history that stretches back over 750 years, its charter having been granted by King Henry III in 1226. In the first part of the 20th century livestock was still sold in the Market Place, as seen here around 1910, but in the early 1920s a separate cattle market came into use. This closed in June 1988, and today its location is part of the Waitrose site. However, the Market Place is still the home of a lively Wednesday morning street market, which is popular with both locals and visitors.

The Jubilee Lamp, beneath which sheep and pigs were once penned, remains the centrepiece of the site, while the buildings in the background are remarkably little changed. Note, however, that the former Red Lion Inn is now called 'Finn M'Cóul's', a manifestation of the modern trend for renamed 'theme pubs'. *Classic Pictures/CH*

The Bridge Garage and Avon Workshop, Ringwood.

WEST STREET, RINGWOOD: The newspaper placard 'Fulham By-Election Sensation' enables us to date the 'past' photograph of Ringwood's West Street to October 1933. In that contest the Conservative candidate, who advocated an increase in the strength of the armed forces and who defended a majority of 14,521, was defeated by the Labour candidate who accused him of being a warmonger; Labour won by a majority of 4,840.

In 1933 West Street was, as its name implies, the main road leading westwards out of Ringwood. The Avon Workshop can be seen in the centre of the 1933 photograph; between 1929 and 1937 this was owned by a Mr Charles Purbrook, who made and sold garden ornaments, examples of which can be seen on the forecourt. In the 1999 photograph it has become the Avon Angling Centre, while what was Mr Kerley's tobacconist and newsagent next door has become a shop called 'Fair Deal'. The Bridge Garage has long gone, and the site is now occupied by Wilts & Dorset's Ringwood Bus Depot. *Classic Pictures/CH*

HIGH STREET, ASHLEY HEATH: During the 1920s Mr William Webb, who originated from Surrey, acquired over 1,500 acres of land at Ashley Heath, near Ringwood, which he laid out as a garden estate. Each residence was situated in at least an acre of land, which was planted with trees and shrubs. The railway line from Brockenhurst to Poole via Ringwood and Wimborne passed nearby, and Mr Webb persuaded the Southern Railway to provide a station to serve the new estate. This opened on 1 April 1927 and closed with the line from 4 May 1964. Mr Webb was also aware of the need for local shops to supply food and other essentials to the residents of his new estate, and therefore included what has been described as the smallest High Street in the country. It consists in its entirety of this short row of shops, seen here newly built and in 1999. Underneath the clock is the inscription 'The Night Cometh'; Mr Webb was aware of the need for people to have a good night's rest, and the chimes of the clock were apparently silenced from 10pm until 7am each day.

The shops originally in the High Street included a grocer and general store, a haberdashery and a Post Office. Today a pharmacy occupies the two middle units with a hairdresser at the far end. The unit nearest the camera

became the Cherry Tree Montessori School in June 1995, providing a method of education originated in Italy by Maria Montessori, which encourages each child to fulfil his or her maximum individual potential. Learning through discovery is encouraged, with the teachers seen as friends and guides. The Cherry Tree School caters for 60 youngsters aged between two and four years, who afterwards continue their education at various local schools. *Classic Pictures/CH*

SALISBURY STREET, FORDINGBRIDGE: The pleasant country town of Fordingbridge was noted in the Domesday Book and derives its title from 'forde' and 'bridge'. The photographs compare Salisbury Street in 1925 and 1999. The Post Office seen in the right foreground of the 1925 photograph, with a smiling and smartly uniformed postman on his bicycle outside, was opened that year, replacing an earlier Post Office located in the High Street from 1884, which by all accounts would seem to have been a delightfully antiquated shop. No doubt the 1925 shop seemed right up to date by comparison. When the Post Office was again moved to modern purpose-built premises on the other side of the street, Barclays Bank took over this building for its Fordingbridge branch. The next shop along the road is still a butcher in 1999, but it will be noted that carcasses no longer hang outside the shop! The large house in the background facing the camera is the Old Court House of the Manor of Burgate, built in 1711. The windows were replaced during the 1940s, slightly altering the appearance of the building.

Traffic is a feature of the modern photograph, taken on a weekday afternoon in June 1999, despite Fordingbridge having gained a bypass in the mid-1970s. *Classic Pictures/CH*

BAT & BALL, BREAMORE: Breamore is an interesting village that has remained singularly free of modern development. Now a conservation area, it is hoped that Breamore will retain its historic charm for years to come. The Bat & Ball public house is beside the main A338 Ringwood to Salisbury road, which runs through the village. This busy main road now has an asphalt surface, but at this point is no wider than it was in 1900. The inn takes its name from the game of cricket, which was already being played in the village when the public house was established in 1830.

Some fencing has been removed to make more room for a car parking area, but the main building has changed very little in the almost 100 years that separate the two photographs. Note, however, the unusual inn sign in the modern view depicting an early cricket player; it is based on a painting 'The Boy with the Bat', which can be seen in nearby Breamore House (open to the public at certain times and well worth a visit). *Classic Pictures/CH*

THE BOROUGH, DOWNTON: The original settlement at Downton, which dates back to Saxon and Norman times, was to the east of the River Avon. In the 13th century the then Bishop of Winchester planned and had built a new borough on the west of the river to extend the town, and this area is still known as The Borough. These photographs compare The Borough in around 1910 and 1999. What is immediately apparent is the number of parked cars and the complete lack of pedestrians in the June 1999 photograph. A number of people can be seen in the earlier photograph, and in those days there was no need for them to be segregated from what little traffic there was by a pavement!

The shop front in the left foreground has been simplified and different merchandise is now sold, while a modern bungalow has been built on the right. In most other respects there have been few changes at this rather attractive location. Note the cottage in the process of being rethatched in the present-day photograph. *Classic Pictures/CH*

Salisbury and Wiltshire

MARKET SQUARE, SALISBURY: Tuesday and Saturday markets are still held in the central Market Square in Salisbury, but for many years have consisted of produce and general goods, the livestock market having moved to another site in the years following the Second World War. The 'past' photograph illustrates a Tuesday market around 1900. The cages on trestles in the centre hold poultry, and in front of them sheep are being sold in the auctioneer's ring.

When the 1900 photograph is compared with the modern view it is immediately apparent how little the buildings surrounding the Market Square have changed, although most now have different commercial uses. On Wednesday 26 August 1998 the Wilts & Dorset Bus Company placed 16 Optare Solo single-deck buses and three low-floor Optare Spectra double-deck buses (see pages 83, 84 and 88) on display in the Market Square. An official launch ceremony took place later that morning and the following week Salisbury became the first place in the United Kingdom to achieve a city-wide network of easy access bus services. Notice how the trees have grown in 98 years! *Classic Pictures/Richard Weaver*

CASTLE STREET, SALISBURY: Salisbury, or the City of New Sarum, is situated 200 feet above sea level at the confluence of four rivers, the Avon, the Nadder, the Bourne and the Wylye. An early exercise in town planning that took place when the city was established following the completion of work on the present Cathedral in 1258, Salisbury's main streets are laid out in parallel north to south and east to west, forming a chequer pattern around the Market Square. Castle Street is one of the main thoroughfares leading northwards from the Market Square. At the time of the 'past' photograph, dating from 1918, it was clearly safe to stroll along the middle of the street or to stand in the roadway with a bicycle and chat. The amount of traffic in the 'present' view, taken on an August evening in 1999, indicates that such actions would now be rather foolish...

The buildings in the left foreground of the 1918 view, including the 'Sheppard High Class Registry Office for Servants', have been replaced by the Tesco supermarket with modern offices above, but some of the buildings seen in the earlier view survive further along the street. *Classic Pictures/CH*

HIGH STREET, BULFORD: In the 1891 Census Bulford village had a population of 341; this was a decline from 408 in 1851, and virtually all the residents were locally born and bred. But this was soon to change as a result of Government policy. By the 1890s it was apparent that the Army needed more land of its own, and the Wiltshire Downlands appeared very suitable as training grounds for the military strategies of the time. Under the provisions of the Military Lands Act, 1892, some 2,956 acres were purchased at Bulford in 1897; subsequently the military authorities have acquired huge tracts of Salisbury Plain for training purposes.

The original Bulford Post Office had been further along the High Street, but was moved to the premises seen here, which were built by the WD Land Agent, when the old building was demolished. The photographs compare the building in the 1950s and in 1999. It is still the Post Office today, but the signage now gives greater prominence to its general store role. Apart from the extension at the far end, changes to the building have been largely superficial. The wall-mounted postbox, partly hidden by a fence-post in the 1950s view, remains, but the general surroundings do appear rather more urbanised in 1999. Note the old 'flaming torch' road sign for the school in the earlier photograph. *Classic Pictures/CH*

RIVER STREET, PEWSEY: Pewsey is a large village that has many of the characteristics of a small town. It was never a borough and never had its own Mayor or Town Council, but with its comprehensive school and variety of shops it is easy to think of Pewsey as a town. However, the visual impression given is certainly village-like. These photographs show River Street in the 1920s and in 1999. The buildings on the right have changed very little, and a traveller returning to Pewsey after an absence of many years would have no difficulty in recognising the place. Notice, however, the differences in the use of the shops; what was Saunders' 'General Warehouse' is now an estate agent, while the former tobacconist next door is now a boutique. The 'Motor Agency' garage on the left, no doubt the height of modernity when the 1920s photograph was taken, has disappeared by 1999! The willow tree in the left foreground adds a pleasant touch to the 1999 scene, taken on a hot Saturday afternoon in **August.** *Classic Pictures/CH*

HIGH STREET, MARLBOROUGH: Marlborough stands 430 feet above sea level in a fold of the downs, and for many centuries has been a stopping point on the road between London and Bath. The High Street is one of the widest streets in England. A huge fire occurred here in 1653 which destroyed 250 houses; however, within a year the town had largely been rebuilt, and some of the present buildings in the High Street date from 1654, although mostly they have been considerably modified. The Town Hall, which is seen in the centre of both photographs, was built in 1900-02 and replaced an earlier building on the same site.

The centre of the High Street was designated for parking in 1926, but is still at times used in its original role as a market, as seen in the photograph taken on a Saturday afternoon in August 1999. The cars in this view are considerably more modern than those seen in the 1930s scene, and the shop fronts on the left have been updated, although sections of the covered area in front of the shops remain. On the far right of the photographs the former Ailesbury Arms Hotel has been converted for use as offices and is now known as Ailesbury Court. Purpose-designed as a hotel, the building dates from the 1840s, and in its day was one of the leading hotels in the area.
Classic Pictures/CH

SOUTH STREET, BROAD CHALKE: Broad Chalke is a delightful village that nestles in the valley of the River Ebble (often called the Chalke Valley) about 8 miles west of Salisbury. A number of famous people have lived in the village, including Cecil Beaton and Sir Anthony Eden.

The main building seen in the photographs was for many years the village Post Office, and it can be seen that it has been considerably altered over the years. The postbox, formerly built into the wall of the building as seen in this 1920s photograph, was relocated to its own brick-built pillar in the 1950s, where it still remains. However, the Post Office closed 1993, and Broad Chalke was without this facility for a few months. Then a Post Office counter was opened in the butcher's shop further along South Street; this remains an excellent village store in 1999, acting as a grocery and greengrocery as well as a butcher and Post Office. Unsurprisingly the arrangement of the doors and windows at the old Post Office has completely changed, and probably only the positioning of the pillar-box would give the casual visitor to the village any clue to the building's former use. *Classic Pictures/CH*

BERWICK ST JOHN: This small, attractive village is situated below Winklebury Hill, which was used as a hill-fort in Iron Age times. In Berwick St John two-storey buildings of stone or rubble with red-brick chimneys are a feature; roofs are thatch, tile or slate.

On the day that the 'past' photograph was taken in around 1910, it seems that many of the younger residents of the village have gathered, while in the background cattle stand contentedly in the road. When the 1999 photograph was taken in the late afternoon of Monday 31 May, no human or animal life was evident, but a number of parked cars can be seen. However, no doubt in both 1910 and 1999 the locals enjoyed refreshment at The Talbot on the left. Notice how the cottages on the right have been 'gentrified'. *Classic Pictures/CH*

Around Dorset

THE CHURCHILL ARMS, ALDERHOLT, takes its name from the Churchill family who occupied Alderholt Park, a large house about a mile north of the village, from the 1850s to the 1920s. The 'past' view dates from around 1904; note the enamel sign on the wall of the stable block advertising J. J. Allen's furniture store in Bournemouth, and the young lad leaning on the wall looking at the pony trap.

Surprisingly little has changed in the modern view, taken in June 1999. Some conversion work has been carried out on the stable block, and the premises as a whole are now very nicely decorated, but a number of features seen in the earlier view can still be identified. The building in the left background in the trees in both views is the original Alderholt Post Office; the present-day facility is on the other side of Station Road. Alderholt has seen very rapid development in recent years, the population rising from around 800 as recently as 1975 to almost 3,000 in 1998. *Classic Pictures/CH*

VERWOOD STATION, on the Salisbury-West Moors line, opened in December 1866. A huge brickworks, the Verwood & Gotham Brick & Tile Company, was established close to the station and was served by its own sidings, bringing coal in and taking bricks and tiles out, until 1945. This was one of a number of brickworks in the Verwood area, where there was also a thriving pottery industry.

Verwood Station closed in May 1964, and almost all evidence that the railway once served the town has now been removed. Houses stand where the station, sidings and brickworks once were. The 1920s photograph was taken from the overbridge carrying the B3081 road. In recent years this road has been realigned and now crosses part of the former station site, eliminating the need for the bridge, as can be seen in the modern photograph. Fortunately the redundant bridge remains in situ, enabling the 1999 photograph to be taken from the same location as around 75 years previously. *Classic Pictures/CH*

VERWOOD CROSS ROADS: It was necessary to take the June 1999 photograph of Verwood Cross Roads from a slightly different angle from that used in the mid-1930s to avoid the present-day view being more or less obliterated by the large tree on the right. Nonetheless the main building in both views is instantly recognisable. Hopkins's Newsagents was established at Verwood Cross Roads in the late 1920s; the shop is still a newsagent and is still run by the Hopkins family in 1999. The shop next door, which was Whitemore's ironmongery during the 1930s, is now an estate agent.

A modern flat-roofed extension has replaced the previous structure to the left of Hopkins's, while the large house on the other side of the crossroads has also been replaced. The population of Verwood increased enormously in the last few decades of the 20th century, and by the mid-1990s had reached 11,000. *Classic Pictures/CH*

STATION ROAD, WEST MOORS: A period of around 70 years separates these two photographs. The location is readily recognisable in both views, but a number of detailed changes can be observed. The shops and the garage on the left were put up during the 1920s, and had not long been built at the time of the 'past' photograph; when comparing it with the 1999 view notice the infill development in exactly the same style, almost certainly carried out shortly afterwards.

Originally the garage held a dealership for Morris cars, and cars are still sold from the site in 1999, but petrol retailing has ceased (see also page 94); note the relocation of the garage's canopy. The West Moors area has been considerably built up during the years that separate the photographs, and clearly the 1999 view gives a more urbanised impression – the lack of people and traffic is explained by the fact that the present-day photograph was taken during the middle of a dull June evening. *Classic Pictures/CH*

WEST BOROUGH, WIMBORNE: The attractive market town of Wimborne is dominated by the lovely Minster Church of St Cuthburga, whose two towers can be seen in both photographs; the left-hand tower dates from the 12th century and is the oldest part of the building, while the slightly taller West tower was built in 1464. When comparing the photographs of West Borough, it is remarkable how little the view has altered between 1930 and 1999.

However, one building has seen considerable changes. The large Georgian house on the right of the 1930 photograph was later rebuilt internally and extended at the rear to become the Tivoli Cinema, which opened on 24 August 1936. Sadly this closed in April 1980, and the building stood empty for ten years. Then a group of local people formed the 'Friends of the Tivoli' and on 23 November 1993 it re-opened as the Tivoli Theatre; it is now used for concerts and live theatre as well as cinema presentations. The traffic island, traffic lights and pelican crossings in the foreground of the 1999 photograph date from the early 1980s. *Classic Pictures/CH*

STAPEHILL POST OFFICE: Stapehill is situated between Wimborne and Ferndown, and is best known for the beautiful Stapehill Abbey, which was occupied by Cistercian nuns for 200 years and is now open to the public. The houses seen in these photographs of Stapehill village were built in 1910, and apart from the fitting of replacement windows and the addition of television aerials they have changed little in appearance over the years. The Post Office has had a more modern shop front fitted, although this does blend in with the character of the building. Notice also that the chimney stack has been removed.

The brick-built pillar-box has been replaced by the free-standing metal type, and a Parish Council notice case is now displayed. A bus-stop lay-by has been provided, and pedestrian access to the shop improved. Notice the various brands of cigarettes prominently advertised in the 1940s view – at that time smoking was a very socially acceptable and almost universal habit. Also noticeable in the 'past' photograph is the overhead electricity supply; this was not replaced by underground cables until the mid-1990s. *Classic Pictures/CH*

WINDGREEN, CORFE MULLEN: From the end of the Second World War, and especially from the mid-1960s onwards, considerable residential development has taken place at Corfe Mullen. When the 'past' photograph was taken in the early 1960s the area had quite a rural aspect, but by 1999 the scene has become distinctly suburban.

These photographs are looking north along the B3074 at Windgreen. The roundabout in the foreground of the 1999 view was built in the late 1980s when a new road to the right was opened, serving new housing at Roman Heights and linking Windgreen with the Wimborne Road at Cogdean. This new road thus relieved the formerly busy junction on the B3074 at Lockyer's School, just out of view in the background of the photographs. The school here was opened by Richard Lockyer in 1706 to provide an education for 30 Corfe Mullen children free of charge; there is a still a thriving middle school on the site in 1999. Note the garage on the corner of Wareham Road, which in 1999 sells Esso instead of Cleveland petrol. *Classic Pictures/CH*

GOLD HILL, SHAFTESBURY: Shaftesbury is one of the oldest and highest towns in Dorset, occupying a commanding location overlooking Blackmore Vale. In the 9th century King Alfred founded an abbey here – his daughter was the first abbess – and this became the richest Benedictine nunnery in England. This once great abbey was destroyed at the time of the Dissolution, but parts of the walls remain and can be seen on the right of both of these photographs of Gold Hill, Shaftesbury's best-known thoroughfare.

This steep, cobbled street was made famous by a television commercial for a certain brand of bread, and is now much sought out by tourists. Not surprisingly, there have been few changes between the 1930s and the 1990s, and the one motor car in the present-day photograph looks rather out of place! The little girl looking out of the window in the 1930s scene would be a senior citizen today, but she would have no difficulty in recognising the street of her childhood. *Classic Pictures/CH*

SOUTH STREET, WAREHAM: Although around 90 years separate these two photographs, the location can instantly be recognised. The building in the left foreground is now the Purbeck Angling shop, but in general the buildings on that side of the road are remarkably little changed. Notice the Black Bear Hotel, built around 1770, which features a life-size statue of a black bear on its porch, prominent in both photographs. The clocktower in the right background is a feature of Wareham Town Hall, which was rebuilt in its present form in the 1870s.

Again, many of the buildings on the right can also be seen with few changes in the August 1999 photograph, although those in the foreground of the older picture were demolished in 1926 to allow for road widening. This now provides a glimpse of the original Wareham Police Station on the extreme right, albeit no longer used as such, which was built in 1859 after the formation of the County Constabulary, to a design used for police stations in a number of Dorset towns. *Classic Pictures/CH*

VICTORIA TERRACE, SWANAGE: Swanage originated as a fishing and quarrying village, but was considerably expanded and transformed into a resort during the 19th century, largely due to the efforts of two men, John Mowlem and George Burt, both of whom were important people in the stone industry. The buildings in the centre of both photographs were given the name Victoria Terrace when newly built in 1837. Number 1 Victoria Terrace was owned by the Burt family from new, and in the 'past' photograph, dating from around 1900, it is advertised as Burt's Restaurant and Stores. In 1999 the building has become the White Horse Inn. John Mowlem retired to No 2 next door in 1844.

Almost 100 years separates the two photographs, but the location is still readily identifiable. The Ship Hotel in the right background is no longer used as such, but its outward appearance has changed little. The Swanage Straw Basket Works and Hixson's House Agency in the left foreground were demolished in 1908, but the subsequent replacement has clearly been designed to blend in well with its surroundings. As can be seen, the area still attracts passers by, but the motor car has, of course, long since ousted the pony and carriage. *Classic Pictures/CH*

Transport of delight

BRISTOL K5G BUS: The Bristol K series of buses originated in 1937. Often described as an 'engineer's bus', the K was designed as a rugged, reliable and easily maintained vehicle. By the late 1930s most Bristol buses were bodied by Eastern Coach Works of Lowestoft, and following the nationalisation of the Tilling group in the postwar period Bristol and ECW became a combination as familiar as fish and chips, providing almost all the rolling-stock for the state-owned bus sector.

Prewar Bristol Ks were powered by five-cylinder Gardner engines, and were given the designation K5G. The chassis featured the relatively high KV radiator, and ECW produced as a standard a pleasing lowbridge body of six-bay construction. This is exemplified by these photographs of Hants & Dorset fleet number 1050 (ERU 601), new in March 1939 and photographed in the early 1950s in largely original condition. Notice the half-drop windows and the single-skin upper-deck ceiling. *All Wilts & Dorset collection*

BRISTOL K6A BUS (1948): The Second World War imposed severe restrictions on the supply of new buses, but with the return to peace in 1945 energetic steps were taken to provide what were by then desperately needed new vehicles. Postwar Bristol Ks were fitted with the lower PV radiator, while ECW developed a very attractive five-bay body that was fitted as a standard.

Illustrated here is Hants & Dorset fleet number 1158 (HLJ 15), new in March 1948. Like many postwar Bristol Ks, this was fitted with a 7.7-litre AEC engine and was given the designation K6A. Hants & Dorset had a large fleet of Bristol K6As, which were particularly associated with Poole and Bournemouth depots, where they regularly worked on some of the longer routes until 1966-7. Notice the use of varnished wood in the interior and the pleasing overall impression given by this very well-designed and built bus. In my younger days I certainly regarded this batch of vehicles as my favourites, and when travelling with a Day Out Ticket (antecedent to the Explorer or Getaway) I would often make snap changes to my plans to travel on them! *All Wilts & Dorset collection*

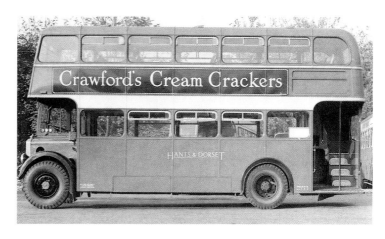

79

BRISTOL K6A BUS (1949): Between May 1948 and June 1949 Hants & Dorset purchased 61 Bristol K6As (fleet numbers 1152-1212) exactly like No 1158 illustrated on the previous page. There followed two batches of, for a Tilling fleet, very non-standard buses – six AEC Regents and six highbridge Leyland Titans. However, from October 1949 deliveries of Bristol Ks resumed. The first five, fleet numbers 1225-1229, were more K6As, but subsequent vehicles were K6Bs (with Bristol AVW engines) or K5Gs.

These photographs show fleet number 1227 (JEL 246), and a number of detail changes to the interior will be noticed when compared with the views of No 1158. Deliveries of lowbridge buses in this later style continued through 1950 into 1951, with the later examples being 27 feet long and 8 feet wide and having the designation KSW. The final lowbridge bus to be delivered to Hants & Dorset was fleet number 1298 (KRU 964), a KSW6B.

I am perhaps a little unusual in that I liked lowbridge buses, even to work on as a conductor – the open rear platform seen in the photograph brings back many happy memories. Lowbridge buses were a feature of the Hants & Dorset and Wilts & Dorset fleets for many years, the last original Hants & Dorset example in public service appropriately enough being KRU 964, which was withdrawn at the end of October 1973. However, some KSW5Gs inherited from the Salisbury-based Wilts & Dorset remained, and when JMW 243 was withdrawn in April 1974 it was the last lowbridge Bristol/ECW bus in service anywhere in the National Bus Company. *All Wilts & Dorset collection*

INTENDING PASSENGERS WAITING
AT A REQUEST STOP
ARE REMINDED THAT THEY SHOULD
SIGNAL THE DRIVER

BRISTOL KSW6B BUS: The Bristol KSW buses delivered to Hants & Dorset during the later part of 1951 and in 1952 were fitted with ECW highbridge bodywork. Although this provided a centre gangway on both decks, the extra height of the bus to accommodate this meant that great care had to be taken to avoid assigning these vehicles to routes with low railway bridges. In all, Hants & Dorset had 38 highbridge KSWs, the first 25 having Bristol engines (KSW6B) while the remaining 13 had the Gardner 6LW unit (KSW6G).

Some of the KSW6Gs went to Hants & Dorset's Eastern Area, but in general the highbridge KSWs were particularly associated with Poole Depot, where they could be found working the trunk routes between Poole and Bournemouth via Upper Parkstone until well into the 1970s. They were popular buses with the crews, and I certainly enjoyed working on them during my time on Hants & Dorset's road staff. The photographs show fleet number 1322 (LRU 51), a KSW6B from the 1952 intake, and nicely illustrate the roomy and comfortable interior. The last of the highbridge KSWs was withdrawn from service in November 1974, but the type is still remembered fondly by many longer-serving staff members. *All Wilts & Dorset collection*

SERVICES : 1, 2, 3, 4, 5, 5A, 6, 7, 8, 9, 10, 11, 14, 22, 26, 29, 31, 32, 33, 34, 34A, 89, 90, 91, 95, and 97.

WORKERS' WEEKLY TICKETS
Borough of Poole

Special weekly tickets available for use only when the outward journey is made each morning by the holder of the ticket boarding a bus at a point where it is scheduled to leave at or before 8.45 a.m. One return journey daily is permitted. These tickets are not issued after 8.45 a.m. on Tuesday of any week.

WEEKLY TICKET RATES

Ordinary Adult Single Fare		6-Day Monday-Saturday		5-Day Monday-Friday
2d.	...	1/6	...	1/3
3d.	...	2/–	...	1/8
3½d.	...	2/6	...	2/1
4d.	...	2/6	...	2/1
4½d.	...	3/–	...	2/6
5d.	...	3/6	...	2/11
5½d.	...	3/6	...	2/11
6d.	...	4/–	...	3/4
7d.	...	4/6	...	3/9
8d.	...	5/–	...	4/2
9d.	...	5/6	...	4/7
10d.	...	6/6	...	5/5
11d.	...	7/6	...	6/3

These tickets can only be used for journeys entirely within the Borough of Poole, or extending from a point in the Borough to any point on either the route between County Gates and Bournemouth Square or the route between Surrey Road and the Square.

BRISTOL LODEKKA BUS: As already seen, from the 1930s until the early 1950s a high proportion of buses were built to the lowbridge design because of restricted height clearances on many routes. Most people disliked them, but buses with a centre gangway on both decks were simply too high to be used in some areas. In its time, therefore, the Bristol Lodekka was revolutionary. An ingenious arrangement of the transmission allowed a slightly sunken gangway on the lower deck, which in turn allowed a centre gangway to be provided on the top deck, while overall the bus was no higher than the former lowbridge design. Eastern Coach Works built a very attractive body for the Lodekka as a standard.

Hants & Dorset received its first Lodekka in April 1953, and large quantities of these versatile buses were delivered in subsequent years. The photographs show fleet number 1341 (LRU 71), an early example that remained in service until the mid-1970s. While there were detail differences in the various batches, the general appearance as far as the customer was concerned remained very similar. One of the more significant changes was that buses delivered from 1960 onwards had virtually flat lower-deck floors, and air rather than vacuum brakes.

Finally, from the mid-1960s the company took delivery of some front-entrance Lodekkas with 70 seats – this was a considerable change to the design, and I thought them less attractive than the previous rear-platform type. The company received its last new Lodekka in 1968, and both rear-platform and front-entrance examples survived in service with Hants & Dorset until 30 November 1980, when all routes were converted to one-man operation.
All Wilts & Dorset collection

OPTARE SPECTRA DOUBLE-DECK BUS: Wilts & Dorset took delivery of its first ten Optare Spectra double-deck buses in April 1993; more have followed, bringing the fleet total of Spectras to 59 by June 2000. Built on a DAF chassis and powered by a DAF RS200L turbocharged engine transversely mounted at the rear, these low-height double-deckers use the highly advanced Alusuisse body construction system.

The standard Wilts & Dorset Spectra is fitted with 77 generously spaced seats, trimmed with Holdsworth moquette to a design unique to Wilts & Dorset. The centre line of the ceiling is also trimmed with this moquette. Features such as large-diameter textured handrails with contrast-coloured bell-pushes, non-slip floor coverings and high-visibility step nosings combine to make journeys easier for all bus-users, especially the elderly, disabled and partially sighted. The interiors of both decks of a standard Optare Spectra are seen here, while the exterior view shows fleet number 3119 (L119 ALJ) at Meeting House Lane, Ringwood, in the summer of 1994. *Wilts & Dorset collection/CH (2)*

OPTARE SPECTRA DOUBLE-DECK BUS: A batch of four Optare Spectras delivered in January 1995 were fitted with 73 semi-coach seats and painted in Wilts & Dorset's coach livery. All four are based at Salisbury, where they are used for private hire work as well as on limited-stop and other bus services. Fleet number 3139 (M139 KRU) poses for the camera at Hale in April 1996, while the close-up view of the comfortable semi-coach seating was taken in September 1999. *Richard Weaver/ CH*

In 1998-9 six low-floor wheelchair-accessible Optare Spectras entered service. These have seats for 76 passengers and incorporate a wheelchair space and buggy zone. They have the lowest entrance step of any double-deck bus in the UK, and all six are based in Salisbury, which in September 1998 became the first place in Britain to achieve a city-wide network of wheelchair-accessible bus services (see also pages 60-61 and 88). A further six easy-access Spectras, allocated to Poole and Lymington depots, were delivered in the early summer of 2000. The photograph shows a crowd of schoolchildren eager to board fleet number 3155 (R155 NPR) in Endless Street, Salisbury, during September 1999. *Chris Allnatt*

BRISTOL L5G BUS: Concurrently with the K series of double-deck buses (see pages 78-80) Bristol also built an equivalent single-deck chassis – the L type. During the period between July 1938 and March 1940 Hants & Dorset took delivery of 37 Bristol L5G buses, all fitted with Beadle bodywork. Shortly after the Second World War the majority of these buses either had their bodywork extensively rebuilt or were fitted with new bodies. They were withdrawn during the 1950s and early 1960s.

These photographs show fleet number 734 (BOW 167), dating from July 1938, in the early 1950s and after its original Beadle body had been rebuilt by Hovis in April 1947. Between October 1947 and September 1948 a further six L5G and six L6A buses with Eastern Coach Works bodies were delivered to Hants & Dorset, together with no fewer than 39 Bristol L coaches with bodywork variously by Beadle, Dutfield and Portsmouth Aviation. Between 1957 and 1962 a number of these coaches were rebuilt as one-man-operated buses, some receiving new full-fronted Eastern Coach Works bodies and surviving in service until the early 1970s. *All Wilts & Dorset collection*

BRISTOL LL6B BUS: From 1 June 1950 the maximum permitted length for a single-deck bus in the United Kingdom was increased to 30 feet. Bristol offered a longer version of its standard chassis, which was designated the LL, or the LWL in the case of the 8-feet-wide version. Hants & Dorset soon took advantage of these longer dimensions, and three dual-purpose saloons with Portsmouth Aviation bodywork were delivered in October 1950, followed in 1951-2 by seven buses with 39-seat rear-entrance Eastern Coach Works bodies. The photographs show fleet number 785, KRU 991, an ECW LL6B dating from 1952, in its original form.

The introduction of one-man operation on single-deck routes, much facilitated by underfloor-engined buses (see opposite), soon made the front-engined half-cab single-deck bus obsolete. In 1960 all seven ECW-bodied LLs were rebuilt with full-fronted forward-entrance bodies and were equipped for one-man operation, in which guise they remained in service until the early 1970s. *All Wilts & Dorset collection*

HANTS & DORSET

OFFICIAL

TIME TABLE

PRICE 1/-

14th June, 1953

UNTIL FURTHER NOTICE

HANTS & DORSET MOTOR SERVICES LIMITED
8 BATH ROAD · BOURNEMOUTH

BRISTOL LS5G BUS: As far back as the 1930s there had been experiments in producing single-deck buses with underfloor engines as a way of increasing passenger capacity. From 1946 onwards Midland Red (who built their own buses) moved entirely to underfloor engines for its new single-deck intake, then in 1950 Bristol and Eastern Coach Works brought out a prototype – the LS – which was to revolutionise the single-deck fleets of the Tilling group companies.

Hants & Dorset took delivery of 20 LS buses and 15 coaches between 1953 and 1957. The first 15 buses were delivered as dual-doorway vehicles and were initially used for crew operation, but by the early 1960s the rear doorway had been removed and they were used as one-man-operated buses. Here we see fleet number 791 (MLJ 143) as built, with ECW body. Many considered the LS more austere in appearance than the earlier LL. This batch of LS vehicles continued in service with Hants & Dorset until the early 1970s. *All Wilts & Dorset collection*

OPTARE SOLO BUS: Over a two-year period starting from the spring of 1998, Wilts & Dorset has invested over £7 million in new easy-access vehicles, including 86 Optare Solo single-deck buses. The company worked closely with Optare Limited of Leeds in the design of the Solo, which has the lowest entrance step of any bus in the UK. These buses set new standards of comfort and accessibility for all passengers, including wheelchair-users and parents with baby buggies. Solos are environmentally friendly, too, with the most advanced engine technology and fitted with catalytic converters.

Two young mothers boarding fleet number 2602 (R602 NFX) in North Road, Poole, demonstrate that it is no longer necessary to take the baby out of the buggy for a bus journey, while the view of the same bus at Burton Green shows the engine access panel at the rear of the vehicle.

In addition to the wheelchair space/buggy zone, the spacious, light and airy interior contains 27 fixed and three tip-up seats. *Ray Humphries (2)/CH*

BEDFORD OB COACH: Hants & Dorset needed a large number of new coaches in the early postwar period, and as would be expected for a Tilling company, 39 Bristol L coaches entered service between July 1947 and August 1950. Then in the summer of 1950 the company took delivery of three coaches of a type very popular at the time with independent rural operators but less associated with the then state-owned sector of the industry.

These three Bedford OB coaches were fitted with Duple bodywork and were originally painted in the cream coach livery. However, by the mid-1950s they had been downgraded to dual-purpose status, and had been repainted in the green bus livery. The photographs show fleet number 685 (KEL 677) at that time, and contrast its bus-style exterior with the comfortable coach-type interior. The exterior view is interesting in that the vehicle is parked in Kingland Road, Poole, at a point that in 1999 would be roughly in the middle of Poole Bus Station; buses parked in the old Bus Station can just be glimpsed in the left background. *All Wilts & Dorset collection*

BRISTOL LS, MW AND RE COACHES: Hants & Dorset's first underfloor-engined coaches entered service in 1953. The initial batch of five were Bristol LS6Gs with just 28 well-spaced seats in their Eastern Coach Works bodies, and were used for extended holiday tours. The photograph shows fleet number 850 (MLJ 145) when new, marked up for a tour of the Scottish Highlands. Later deliveries had 39 seats, with a total of 15 LS coaches being taken into stock between 1953 and 1957.

Eastern Coach Works soon modified the front end of its standard coach body, and the revised form is seen in this photograph of fleet number 869 (YEL 228), a Bristol MW6G dating from 1959. A completely new type of ECW body was fitted to the Bristol MW coaches delivered from 1961 onwards.

SEATING PLAN

In the mid-1960s Bristol developed a single-deck chassis with an underfloor rear-mounted engine – the RE. While the company's RE buses were all bodied by Eastern Coach Works, a number of RE coaches with Duple bodywork also came into the fleet. Here we see fleet number 924 (REL 741H), a Bristol RELH6G with 40-seat Duple Commander bodywork when new in August 1969 at the former Southampton Coach Station at Bedford Place. *Wilts & Dorset collection (2)/L. Harvell, Wilts & Dorset collection*

BOVA AND DAF PLAXTON COACHES: Since 1983 the Wilts & Dorset Bus Company has had a small number of coaches in the fleet. These include three Bova Futura 49-seat vehicles, which were purchased new in December 1993 and delivered in National Express livery for use on the Yeovil-Salisbury-London service operated by Wilts & Dorset. The trio were posed for a publicity photograph at Wilton House on 31 December 1993 prior to taking up their duties on that route. *Richard Weaver*

At the time of writing Wilts & Dorset's latest coaches are five DAF/Plaxton 53-seat vehicles. These photographs show interior and exterior views of fleet number 3216 (T216 REL) at Salisbury Bus Station on the evening of Monday 30 August 1999. These vehicles are used mainly on Service X4 between Salisbury and Bath; the handgrips fitted to the luggage racks allow eight standing passengers to be carried at busy times. Note the special window graphics advertising the route. These comfortable vehicles are also used for private hire duties. *Both CH*

MAUNSELL AND BULLEID 3rd CLASS COMPARTMENT CARRIAGES: Turning now to railway travel, during the period from 1923 until 1936 the Southern Railway built over 1,000 new locomotive-hauled carriages designed by the then Chief Mechanical Engineer, Richard Maunsell. The basic types included both open saloon (ie centre gangway) and compartment carriages, all of which were very comfortable and well-appointed. Here we see the interior of a 3rd Class compartment in carriage 5618, built in 1931, withdrawn from British Rail service in 1965 and now preserved on the Kent & East Sussex Railway. A number of Maunsell carriages ended their days with British Rail operating local services in the area covered by this book (see page 52).

Oliver Bulleid became Chief Mechanical Engineer of the Southern Railway in 1937. His postwar locomotive-hauled stock was spacious, comfortable and modern in appearance; carriages to his designs continued in production until 1951, when the BR Standard Mk 1 carriages started to appear. Here we see the interior of a typical Bulleid 3rd Class compartment in carriage 2515, built in 1951, withdrawn by BR in 1966 and now preserved on the Bluebell Railway in East Sussex. *Both CH*

BULLEID 3rd CLASS AND CLASS 442 OPEN SALOON CARRIAGES: In the first photograph we see the 3rd Class open saloon end of Bulleid carriage 2515. This type of carriage, with a section for luggage and the guard, two 3rd Class compartments (16 seats) and an open saloon with 32 3rd Class seats, was a Bulleid innovation, and together with other types was produced in quantity until 1951, following a survey of passenger requirements in 1945-6. Bulleid carriages continued in general use on fast trains on the Waterloo-Bournemouth-Weymouth and Waterloo-Salisbury-Exeter lines until 1967, well after pre-nationalisation-type carriages on most other main lines had been ousted by BR Standard rolling-stock.

With electrification from Waterloo to Bournemouth in 1967 came 4TC trailer units rebuilt from former steam-hauled BR Standard Mk 1 carriages together with 4REP powered units newly built in 1966-7 to the Mk 1 design. Then electrification onwards to Weymouth in 1988 saw the introduction of the Class 442 'Wessex Electric' units, which incorporate traction equipment recovered from the former 4REP units. The Class 442 units now operate the bulk of the services on the Waterloo-Bournemouth-Weymouth line. All Standard Class accommodation is in open saloons, and the bright and comfortable if somewhat plastic-looking interior of a driving trailer carriage is illustrated here. *Both CH*

REFUELLING THE CAR: At the end of the Second World War less than 10 per cent of the population had access to a motor car. However, with petrol coming off ration from 1950 and the consumer boom that culminated in the 'never had it so good' era, there was a massive increase in car ownership and use that continued unabated to the end of the 20th century.

Here we see a family watching as their car is refuelled at Walkford Garage in the late 1940s. At the same location on Friday 3 September 1999 young Tim Foster watches as the garage attendant fills up the author's car with unleaded petrol – a comparatively recent innovation. It can be seen how the garage premises have been extended and modernised, mostly during the 1950s. Yet Walkford Garage, with its friendly attendant service, is by 1999 old-fashioned. For a number of years the trend has been towards self-service garage forecourts, and in addition supermarkets have come into the field of petrol retailing. The author is seen refuelling his car at a supermarket early in the morning on Saturday 16 October 1999. *Classic Pictures/Rachel Hawker/CH*

ALL DRESSED UP, WITH SOMEWHERE TO GO...: Finally, a comparison of two families going for a day out in a local park. In the first photograph, taken in October 1954, we see Stanley and Mamie Connell with their children, 1-year-old Janice (in the pushchair) and 3-year-old Alan. Notice that even for an outing to the park father is wearing a collar and tie together with a rather formal suit, while his wife's raincoat would be equally appropriate for a trip to a good restaurant.

On Saturday 13 November 1999 Rob and Yolande Hart were photographed with their children Jonathan, aged 4 months, and 3-year-old Sophie at Constitution Hill in Poole. Their more relaxed and casual attire is actually more suitable for an excursion of this nature, and the fashions of the 1990s are in many ways more interesting than the rather fixed attitude that men especially had towards sartorial matters in the 1950s. In particular notice Rob's trainers, a type of footwear now almost universal, and more comfortable and appropriate for this kind of family outing than Stanley's town shoes.

But fashion aside, what has not changed, and what is apparent in both of these photographs, is the delight of a family day out together – a great time on the day, and part of a store of happy memories for the future. *Lisa Connell/CH*

Index of locations

102	RINGWOOD—LOWER MANNINGTON—LOWER ROW—WIMBORNE—COWGROVE							102			
53 T 18/5	Light figures denote a.m. times. Dark figures denote p.m. times										
	TUESDAYS ONLY										
Ringwood (Market Place) ... dep	9 15	...	...	...	...	Cowgrove ... ... dep	1025	1240	2 40	...	...
Ashley Heath Turning ... „	9 18	...	...	...	...	Wimborne (Square) ... arr	1030	1245	2 45	...	...
Three Legged Cross ... ... „	9 30	...	...	...	...	Wimborne (Square) ... dep			2 50	...	...
Mannington (Clumphill) ... „	9 35	...	...	...	...	Colehill (Post Office) ... „	...	...	2 58	...	...
Lower Mannington ... ... „	9 42	...	...	...	...	Broomhill ... ... „	...	...	3 5	...	...
Lower Row ... ... „	9 50	...	...	...	...	Holt Church ... ... „	...	...	3 8	...	...
Holt Church ... ... „	9 54	...	...	...	...	Lower Row ... ... „	...	...	3 12	...	...
Broomhill ... ... „	9 57	...	...	...	...	Lower Mannington ... ... „	...	...	3 20	...	...
Colehill (Post Office) ... „	10 4	...	...	...	...	Mannington (Clumphill) ... „	...	...	3 27	...	...
Wimborne (Square) ... arr	1012	...	...	...	...	Three Legged Cross ... ... „	...	...	3 32	...	...
Wimborne (Square) ... dep	1015	1230	2 30	...	...	Ashley Heath Turning ... „	...	...	3 44	...	...
Cowgrove ... ... arr	1020	1235	2 35	...	...	Ringwood (Market Place) ... arr	...	...	3 47	...	...

PLEASE   ASSIST   THE   CONDUCTING   STAFF

BY   TENDERING

THE CORRECT MONEY

WHEN   PAYING   YOUR   FARE

1958